This book is to be returned
the last date stamped

3 1 OCT 1994

perceptions of the
PICTS:
from Eumenius
to John Buchan

ANNA RITCHIE

ISBN 0 9515778 4 0

Acknowledgements

I should like to acknowledge with gratitude the help of my father-in-law, W F Ritchie, who has listed the references to the Picts and to body-painting in the works of classical authors, and who translated the more obscure and lesser known sources that I have used. I am indebted to Geoffrey Stell for drawing my attention to the Darnaway carvings and for allowing me to read the results of his work at Darnaway prior to publication. Trevor Watkins used the Leydenfrost illustration of Buchan's Galloway Pict in a stimulating lecture on Pictish settlement archaeology (1984), and he was kind enough to lend me the volume from which fig 13 is taken. Iseabail Macleod of the Scottish National Dictionary was very helpful in my search for the vernacular uses of the term Pict, for which I am grateful. Dr Jack Burt was kind enough to draw the Eassie cross-slab specially for the cover of this publication, and the author and Groam House Museum Trust are very grateful to him.

I should like to thank the Trustees of Groam House Museum and their Honorary Curator, Mrs Elizabeth Marshall and assistant Susan Seright, both for the invitation to deliver this lecture and for their warm welcome and hospitality in Rosemarkie in April 1993.

Printed by A4 Print, Inverness.
Produced by Groam House Museum.

Introduction

The last twenty years have seen a great upsurge of interest in the Picts, as the creation of the Groam House Museum and the founding of the Pictish Arts Society testify. This is not a new phenomenon, although previous episodes of interest have not proved as productive. The Picts have exercised a fascination over their descendants virtually since Pictland became Scotland, and it is possible to trace the way in which myths about them evolved and the way in which perception of their character has altered and developed over the centuries. When the Trustees and Committee of Groam House honoured me with the invitation to give this lecture, it seemed to me to be an opportunity to carry out some research into the history of Pictish studies, an aspect in which I have been interested for some time.

In studying the way in which ideas about the Picts have evolved, the last seventeen hundred years can usefully be divided into four blocks of time. The contemporary works of classical and ecclesiastical authors form the first block, from Eumenius in AD 297 to Nennius around 800. The second block takes us from the 9th century to the discovery of the New World in the 16th century, a long way from Pictland but highly influential for ideas about the Noble Savage. The three hundred years from John White's drawings of the late 16th century to the work of Joseph Anderson in the late 19th century form the third block of time, and the fourth brings us via John Buchan to the present day. Each of these periods has a flavour of its own in thinking about the Picts. Among antiquaries of the early 20th century there has been a depressing tendency to duplicate through ignorance the work of the previous century.

A number of themes emerge from a study of the authors and artists concerned with the Picts, some of which are constant and others sporadic. Directly involved with the Picts themselves are the themes of racial origins, language, physical appearance, costume and the question of the Picts in Galloway. Other themes centre round the artefacts attributed to the Picts, from heather ale to 'Pictish Towers', most of which develop after 1700. It was only then that the term *Picti* acquired a cultural connotation.

The trail begins with the works of Roman historians, geographers and poets. The best brief commentary on these early sources remains that of Marjorie Anderson (1973,125-8; see also Anderson 1987).

Classical perception of the Picts

Britain lay on the periphery of the known world in Roman times and indeed until the Viking Age. Vergil's description is typical of the Roman concept of Britain: *'and the Britons, wholly set apart from the whole world' (Eclogues,I,66)*. By the first century AD, the existence of Britain and something of the character of its land and people was well-known to educated Greeks and Romans from the works of authors such as Ptolemy, Strabo and Caesar, and the account of the voyage of the Massiliote Pytheas, now known to us only from quotations in other sources. Polybius and Strabo derided him, but Timaeus and Eratosthenes each took parts of his accounts seriously. Some of these authors had visited Britain themselves, while others merely repeated the descriptions given by earlier writers.

Writing the *Agricola* in AD 97-8, Tacitus considered himself to be a cut above the rest on the grounds that only in his day had the conquest of Britain been completed and knowledge of Britain thereby extended. *'Where my predecessors relied on style to adorn their guesses, I shall offer assured fact' (Agricola,10)*. Tacitus had the advantage of course of being Agricola's son-in-law and being able to talk to the man who led the Roman army into Scotland in AD 79: *'I have often heard Agricola say ...' (Agricola,24)*. It is unfortunate that Tacitus did not record many of his father-in-law's observations about Britain, but one at least became firmly entrenched into modern times - that the Caledonians had *'reddish hair and large limbs' (Agricola,11)*. This was repeated almost 500 years later by Jordanes, and the red hair at least was picked up again by early antiquarians; in a paper read to the London Society of Antiquaries in 1767, J Walker of Moffat claimed that red hair was a sign of Pictish descent (1804,256). The notion passed into common tradition and was recorded for instance in Fife in 1905, when Picts were held to have been *'short wee men wi' red hair and long arms' (Scottish National Dictionary)*. By then two traditions had combined, Tacitus' red hair with a later myth of tiny stature to which I shall return.

Only four Roman writers mention the Picts by name. The first was Eumenius, composing a poem in praise of the emperor Constantius Chlorus in AD 297; he compares Constantius' achievement in Britain with the easier task that faced Julius Caesar in dealing with the Britons, *'a nation, still savage and accustomed only to the hitherto semi-naked Picts and Hibernians as their enemies, yielded to Roman arms and standards without difficulty'*. Mrs Anderson pointed out that the use here of the name *Picti* is anachronistic (1973,125), a point which Alfred Smyth took to mean that Eumenius, quite rightly in Smyth's view, assumed the Picts to have been around in Caesar's day (1984,52). It seems to me equally if not more likely that Eumenius used the term *Picti* simply because it was familiar to his audience in 297, who would understand it to mean the people who lived in the far north of Britain, just as they would understand the Hibernians to be the people of Ireland. Eumenius' description 'hitherto semi-naked' is, however, a reference to the past, and it implies that the Picts no longer fought, as did their Celtic forebears, in their birthday suits.

Another panegyric to Constantius mentions *'the Caledonians and other Picts'*; it was written in 310 but the author is unknown. More informative is the work of the respected historian, Ammianus Marcellinus, in the late third century, although it has been suggested that even he derived his information about the Picts from a panegyric source (Chadwick 1958). Writing of events in the 360s, he describes how *'the savage tribes'* of the Picts and Scots *'harassed the Britons with incessant raids'*, and records that the Picts involved in the raids were *'divided into two tribes, the Dicalydones and the Verturiones'* (21.1,26.4-5,27.8). Clearly, to Ammianus Marcellinus as to Romans generally, the Picts were simply barbarians and further details were unnecessary.

Painted Picts?

The fourth author to mention the Picts specifically was the poet Claudius Claudianus, who wrote at the beginning of the 5th century of the achievements in Britain of the general Stilicho. He casts Britain as a female figure, *'clothed in the skin of a Caledonian beast, her cheeks tattooed, a deep blue cloak sweeping down to her feet'*, who praises Stilicho, *'thanks to his care, I need not fear the arms of the Scots nor tremble at the Picts nor keep watch on all the shores for the coming of the Saxons, no matter what the winds'* (*de laudibus Stilichonis*,2,247). In another poem about Stilicho suppressing a rebellion in Italy, Claudian refers to *'the legion which had been left to guard far-distant Britain, which had kept the fierce Scots in check and gazed at the strange shapes* *tattooed on the faces of the dying Picts' (de bello Gothico,*416-18). In both cases, the term translated as 'tattooed' is literally 'iron-marked' *(ferro picta, ferroque notatas)* suggesting the use of an iron needle rather than simply body-painting. This is the only classical source which attributes either tattooing or body-painting specifically to the Picts, and it should be considered in the context of other classical references to the practice of body-painting among barbarians (eg Caesar, Mela, Martial, Herodotus, Pliny, Solinus). The practice was part of the civilised world's perception of a typical barbarian and as such should not be taken too literally. Claudian was the last great poet of the heathen world, and, because his works were an essential part of the Latin education of the early antiquaries, his influence was strong out of all proportion in perpetuating the concept of the 'iron-marked Pict'.

In addition to Claudian's influence in later times, 6th and 7th century writers such as Jordanes and Isidore of Seville repeated information about tattooing from earlier writers. Isidore adds new detail which has been much discussed in this century. *'The race of the Picts has a name derived from the appearance of their bodies. These are played upon by a needle working with small pricks and by the squeezed-out sap of a native plant, so that they bear the resultant marks according to the personal rank of the individual, their painted limbs being tattooed to show their high birth' (Origines,*19.23.7). There is nothing new to add to the published discussions of the word *Picti* (Chadwick 1958; Anderson 1987); current opinion favours a derivation from the Picts' own name for themselves rather than the nickname 'the painted ones'. Thomas linked the Isidore account with Pictish symbols to suggest that the latter, on memorial stones, recorded the rank of individuals (1963). Even if Isidore's source was truly writing of the Picts, tattooing was no longer practised at the time at which he was writing, around 600, otherwise Adomnan or later Bede would have mentioned such an extraordinary custom.

Nevertheless, the perception of the Picts as painted or tattooed was revived at the Renaissance as scholars rediscovered the classical authors. It was then reinforced in the late 16th century by observations of contemporary body-painting among American Indians, and, as Stuart Piggott has described, *'woad-painted Britons became a literary commonplace'* (1989,63). Wonderful images of painted Picts as well as ancient Britons were devised by John White and Jacques le Moyne de

5

Morgues in the late 16th century, though Piggott has suggested that both were basing their drawings on those in a lost Scottish source (1989,76,82). John White had accompanied Sir Walter Raleigh on his expedition to Virginia in 1585 and saw for himself the American Indians, and Jacques le Moyne had been on the earlier and abortive Florida expedition. Their flamboyant painted Picts, published at the same time as the American drawings, had a lasting impact upon the popular concept of savage barbarians (fig. 1).

Fig. 1. 'A yonge dowgter of the Pictes', watercolour by Jacques le Moyne de Morgues (Yale Center for British Art, Paul Mellon Collection).

Contemporary perceptions in Britain

Writing at about the same time as Isidore of Seville but much closer to home was the author of the Gododdin poem, and here the image is one of heroic society rather than savage barbarism. Kenneth Jackson argued that the poem was composed orally soon after the battle of Catraeth around AD 600, although others have suggested a later date. An oddly moving line records the author: *'This is the Gododdin; Aneurin sang it'*. One of the warriors celebrated in the poem was a Pict, Llifiau son of Cian, and possibly another, Bubon, and presumably the warbands accompanying them were composed of Picts (Jackson 1969,103,108,119,125). *'When he attacked in the borderland his fame was renowned, he deserved his wine, the man wearing a gold torque. He marshalled a bright shining array, the bold one; he was in charge of a hundred men, the noble warrior of renowned spirit, the foreign horseman, the young only son of Cian from beyond Bannog. The men of Gododdin do not tell of anyone more harsh than Llifiau when he was on the field of battle'* (Jackson 1969,103). Jackson identified Bannog as the hills in which the Bannock Burn rises, implying that Llifiau was Pictish (1969,6,79). The poet returns to praising the valour of Llifiau twice more, calling him both friend (119) and kinsman (125), suggesting that Llifiau was well-known to him. The young warrior was the epitome of heroic society, of noble birth and *'dauntless in battle'*. The Gododdin has a rich store of animal imagery which provides a useful background to the animals carved on symbol stones; fierce animals such as the boar, wolf, bull and lion are evoked to convey the valour of the warriors. Death is portrayed as *'the food of ravens'* (126), the raven being not only a carrion bird but also, in Celtic mythology, the incarnation of the goddess of war.

But at this period a writer's perception of the Picts depended upon his political affiliations. Gildas, writing some sixty years earlier than Aneurin, presents an entirely different image of the Picts, but the purpose of his impassioned prose was also entirely different. He was a Welsh monk delivering a lament for the parlous state of Britain after the withdrawal of Roman protection, leaving his country open to the depredations of *'two savage peoples from across the sea'* (transmarinus), the Scots from the north-west and the Picts from the north-east, later described as *'the foul hordes of Scots and Picts'* (*De excidio et conquestu Britanniae*, 19). He compares them to *'dark armies of worms from the narrowest openings of their caves'*, and attributes to them a common *'lust for bloodshed, rather covering their villainous faces with hair than their private parts and the regions nearest them with clothes'*. At this point Gildas would surely have made some contemptuous reference to Pictish tattoos had the practice existed.

It must also be remembered that Gildas was a Christian monk writing of heathens and that this fact coloured his perception of them. Another British Christian whose perception was similarly coloured is reflected in the Letter of St Patrick, which, written in the 5th century, berated the *'most shameful, wicked and apostate Picts'* for buying converted Irish slaves.

In contrast to Gildas and closer to Aneurin is Adomnan's record of the Picts encountered by St Columba. His laudatory biography of Columba was written in the late 7th century, and the sparse details that it offers about the Picts portray a pagan but civilised people. Even the Pictish king's magicians appear restrained in their efforts to combat the threat of Christianity (*Life of Columba*,I,37; II,32-4). By the time that Adomnan was writing, of course, the conversion of the Picts was well underway, but there is no suggestion that in Columba's time they had been any more barbarous in behaviour. Both Adomnan and Bede mention slaves in connection with the Picts, but slavery was an accepted part of life even in the Christian world at this time. Bede provides a tiny cameo of the Pictish royal court in the early 8th century (*Historia Ecclesiastica Gentis Anglorum,* V.21). Abbot Ceolfrith's reply to King Nechtan's request for advice about Easter and the tonsure was *'read in the presence of King Nechtan and many of his more learned men'* together with *'his assembled chieftains'*.

The monastic annals compiled on Iona and in Ireland are too brief to afford any insights into ideas about the Picts. Amongst the exquisite drawings decorating the Book of Kells are many hints that the artist was familiar with the work of Pictish sculptors and with the Picts themselves (Henderson 1986, Brown 1972). Parallels between Pictish symbols and the Evangelists' symbols are well known, and there are other similarities among the minor details of the manuscript. The crouched warrior slipped in at the end of a line on folio 200R (fig. 2) resembles closely the striding warrior on the Eassie cross-slab from

Fig 2. Detail of warrior from the Book of Kells, f.200R (courtesy of The Board of Trinity College, Dublin).

Fig 3. Warrior on the Pictish symbol stone at Eassie, Angus (drawing by Jack Burt).

Angus (fig. 3), both with short haircuts, dressed in breeches and armed with spear and small shield, and the style of the cloak or blanket of the Eassie warrior is echoed on folio 89R by that of a horseman who, to fit in between the lines of writing, seems to have slipped somewhat from the horse's back (fig. 4).

Fig. 4. Detail of horseman from the Book of Kells, f.89R (courtesy The Board of Trinity College, Dublin).

Most interesting of all is the detail on the top right of the opening of St Mark's gospel, folio 130R. This wholly Pictish-looking figure with his beard and formal hair-style appears to be naked and covered with body-painting (fig. 5). Is this a gentle monkish joke, a play on the name of the Picts?

Fig. 5. Detail from the opening to the gospel of St Mark, Book of Kells, f.130R (courtesy of The Board of Trinity College, Dublin).

The Picts' perception of themselves

Nothing has survived of any undoubted Pictish manuscripts, other than the king-lists. The only way in which an impression can be built up of the Picts' perception of themselves is by studying the human images on symbol stones and metalwork. Many figures on the stones are those of clerics in their hooded habits, but there are also secular subjects, largely drawn from the upper echelons of society. Scenes of the landowning classes at play in the hunt flit across the backs of cross-slabs, with fine well-schooled horses and trained hounds. The lost slab from Meigle (no 10), which may have been part of an architectural frieze, shows a swiftly passing horse-drawn carriage with driver and passengers, an image of wealth and social status that Jane Austen would have recognised (fig. 6). Perhaps the most powerful image of power and hierarchy is the carving of three warriors in ceremonial robes on the Brough of Birsay stone from Orkney, for these are men of substance who know their place in the world (fig. 7).

Fig. 6. Horse-drawn carriage from Meigle no.10, Perthshire (Chalmers, P 1848, The Ancient Sculptured Monuments of the County of Angus, Bannatyne Club, pl 18).

Fig. 7. Warriors from the Pictish symbol stone from the Brough of Birsay, Orkney (Crown Copyright, Historic Scotland).

The question arises of whether such figures are themselves symbols or depictions of real people; there is nothing to match the Birsay scene in the repertoire of Pictish stones, and it is tempting to cast them as local dignitaries to whom, if only we had the documentation, names and dates could be given (Ritchie 1983,52). The style of the carving may be more stereotyped. With a very few exceptions, human figures are shown in profile with strong features, and the oval eye, nose and beard of each of the Birsay warriors can be seen in greater detail on the portrait incised on a piece of slate from Jarlshof in Shetland (fig. 8).

Fig. 8. Portrait of a man from Jarlshof, Shetland (Crown Copyright, Historic Scotland).

Here the moustache is clear, a neat moustache rather than the luxuriant drooping-handle affairs sported by warriors on later monuments in Perthshire and Tayside (eg Dupplin, Benvie). The Birsay chieftain and the Jarlshof man share the same hairstyle with formal curls, and a few such curls appear on the cloaked figure on the stone from Burness in Orkney (fig. 9).

Fig. 9. Cloaked figure from the stone from Burness, Orkney.

A stronger hint of stylistic stereotyping arises with the worried frowns of the faces on the Golspie pin from Sutherland and the so-called whetstone from Portsoy in Banffshire (Close-Brooks 1975, pl 27,a and b). Human faces adorn Irish metalwork and stonecarving of the 7th and 8th centuries found in Scotland (eg Crieff mount, Youngs 1989, no 117b; Riasg Buidhe cross, RCAHMS 1984, no 389), but the pronounced lines across the forehead are a Pictish touch. Was this a recognised attribute of a particular figure from Pictish mythology? Such figures can be identified on the stones from Golspie and Rhynie (Aberdeenshire) by their exaggerated facial features and from Papil and Mail in Shetland by their bird and wolf masks, and in all four cases an axe was clearly considered to be an essential accessory (fig. 10).

Fig. 10. Figures from the stones from Rhynie, Golspie and Mail.

Throughout the four hundred years or so of Pictish stone-carving, there must have been an equivalent tradition of wood-carving. It has been suggested that the prototypes of symbol stones may have been wooden (Close-Brooks 1984,107), and it is impossible to conceive that the Pictish love of design and, no doubt, colour was not also expressed in textiles, as furnishings and clothing, and in wood, as furniture, domestic utensils, house-posts and other artefacts. A glimpse of what may have existed can be seen at Darnaway Castle in Moray (Stell & Baillie 1993). The great hall at Darnaway, known as Randolph's Hall, has one of the few surviving medieval timber roofs, which is now known through dendrochronological analysis to be the earliest surviving of such roofs. On the evidence of the tree-rings in the great oak timbers of the roof, the trees of the famous Moray forest which provided the timber were felled in the summer of 1387. Oak must be worked before it hardens, and the roof must have been in place within a few years.

The roof is inhabited, in Geoffrey Stell's words, by *'a world of human figures, beasts, birds and naturalistic carvings'*, including, on one of the main trusses, carvings with a remarkably Pictish flavour.

Beneath a familiar pair of cloaked and hooded clerics, there is a hunting scene consisting of an archer confronting a large creature of the forest with a long tail (fig. 11). These figures were carved more than five hundred years after Pictland became Scotland, but the people's basic life-style would not have changed much and in the forested lands of Moray the age-old preoccupation with hunting was still strong.

Fig. 11. Archer from the roof of the Great Hall at Darnaway Castle, Moray (Crown Copyright, Royal Commission on the Ancient and Historical Monuments of Scotland).

The language and origins of the Picts

The controversy over the Pictish language which has exercised the minds of so many antiquarians and linguists since the 18th century is rooted in the works of Adomnan and Bede, both of whom make it clear that the Picts had a language of their own, though without any real indication of its nature. Most influential of all for later scholarship is Bede's information about the origins of the Picts, another major source of argument over the centuries. The passage in question is too well-known to repeat here (*Historia Ecclesiastica, I,1*) but brings the Picts from Scythia via Ireland to the north of Britain. Bede's source is generally accepted to have been Scottish, since the legend reinforces the Scottish claim to rule Pictland, but Cowan has suggested that there may have been a Pictish interest in promulgating this myth of a common origin for Scots and Picts (1984,125). Nennius, or rather the *Historia Brittonum* which he helped to compile at the beginning of the 9th century, also attributes to the Picts an origin beyond Britain, although he would have them settle first in Orkney.

When the question of Pictish origins was taken up by antiquarians in the early 18th century, their classical education ensured that they understood correctly Bede's Scythia to mean Scandinavia rather than southern Russia. Some accepted Bede's account and continued to do so into the 19th century (eg Dalrymple 1705; Ritson 1828), but others realised that the implications of the works of Roman authors concerning north Britain were that the Picts were originally Celtic. Henry Maule's *History of the Picts* in 1706 identified them as indigenous, as did the highly respected Camden in 1789. Thomas Innes saw their origins as those of the British generally, from Gaul via the short sea crossing from Europe to Britain (1729,71) - and, incidentally, realised that the *Life of St Findan* was evidence for Picts in Orkney (Thomson 1986).

By the start of the 19th century, George Chalmers was able to write *'The lineage of the Pictish people has been disputed, though without any valid reason, as if there could be a doubt whether they were of a Celtic or of a Gothic origin'* (1807, new edition 1887,199), and he traced their lineage from Gauls to Britons to Caledonians and thence to Picts, *'thus changing their names but not their nature'*. Scholars were enjoying the Pictish Controversy, however, and were loth to lose any of the mystery that encouraged endless speculation. Again and again the Celtic ancestry of the Picts had to be argued - half a century later, Daniel Wilson in his Rhind Lectures declared *'We begin to discover that the Northern and Southern Picts, so long the subject of mystery and fable, were no other than the aboriginal Celtae'* (1851,15). Yet, fully a century later, Frederick Wainwright in his preface to *The Problem of the Picts* insisted that *'firm conclusions on the race and origin of the Picts are at present beyond the horizon of attainment'* (1955,11).

Gordon Childe in his volume on *The Prehistory of Scotland* had little to say on the subject, but noted that *'the linguistic and cultural affinities of the Picts are the subjects of bitter and prolonged controversy'*, although the tendency was to treat them as Celts (1935,260,261). Childe might well tread carefully on the subject of the Picts, for his monograph on Skara Brae in 1931 had been subtitled 'a Pictish village in Orkney'; his judgement on the date of this neolithic settlement had been led astray by the coincidental distribution of carved stone balls and Pictish symbol stones. He was then obliged to explain the low technological level of culture at Skara Brae in social terms - the inhabitants were humble people at a degenerate cultural level (1931,164,168-9,181).

Pictish symbol stones

The bible for the study of Pictish stone-carving is the massive tome published by the Society of Antiquaries of Scotland in 1903, *The Early Christian Monuments of Scotland* (and recently re-issued as a facsimile). The authors were Joseph Anderson and J Romilly Allen, and the discussion of the stones was based on Anderson's Rhind Lectures for 1892. It comes as a surprise to realise how reluctant Anderson appears to have been to attribute symbol stones directly to the Picts. His earlier Rhind Lectures of 1880 discussed them at length as Celtic art with only a passing reference to the Picts (1881,200), and only in the 1903 publication did he explicitly relate the distribution of Class I stones to the territory of the Pictish kingdom (cix). Yet by the late 19th century the attribution of symbol stones to the Picts appears to have been generally accepted. The problem for Anderson may have been the fact that other scholars were intent upon proving a Scandinavian origin for the symbols, harking back to Bede's Scythian origin for the Picts.

The Earl of Southesk argued *'Assuming that the Picts were incapable of framing the symbolism without extraneous aid, and that such aid could not have come directly from Orientals, nor from Romans or Celts, whose work elsewhere shows no traces of such a system, or of any system from which it might have been developed, our thoughts are necessarily directed to Scandinavia as the centre of influence.'* (1893,7). He found supporting evidence in the Norse runes on the Monifieth crescentic bronze plaque (1893,80).

The first scholar to argue in print that symbol stones belonged to the Picts had been Daniel Wilson in 1851, and it was taken up by John Stuart in his *Sculptured Stones of Scotland* in 1859; the argument was extended in 1873 by John Alexander Smith to link silver chains with the Picts on the evidence of the symbols on their terminal rings.

The only writer prior to Anthony Jackson (1971; 1984) to consider the cosmology of the Picts was Ludovic Mann in 1915; he drew attention to the swastika of four naked men on the recumbent tombstone (no. 26) at Meigle (fig. 12), attributing the design to a Pictish concept of four quarters in the world. *'The four quarters make a complete circle, and therefore all humanity through love and affinity should join from the four parts and form one inseparable bond of brotherhood'* (1915,142).

Fig. 12. Human swastika from Meigle no 26, Perthshire (Crown Copyright, Royal Commission on the Ancient and Historical Monuments of Scotland).

It is surprising that the Picts with their system of symbols and matrilineal succession failed to attract anthropological interest before the 1970s; after all, Radcliffe-Brown had published influential papers on these and related topics in the 1920s and 1930s (conveniently collected in 1952). Anthony Jackson's work was both timely and provocative, and it is a measure of the average Scottish archaeologist's lack of training in anthropology that Jackson's work appears to have had relatively little impact in terms of direct comment (but see the review by Stephen Driscoll 1986). There is no doubt, however, that it has influenced the way in which late 20th century ideas about the Picts have developed.

Favourite myths

Two of the most enduring of the myths about the Picts are that they were very small in stature and that they lived underground. Both myths can be traced back to the *Historia Norwegiae* written about 1200 by an author whose name is unknown, and the idea of living underground goes back into the 11th century to Adam of Bremen's *History of the Archbishops of Hamburg-Bremen*. In both cases the myths are already just that, myths or folk-tales about a people whose culture had been so successfully either suppressed or adopted by their political overlords, the Scots, from the mid 9th century that the Picts themselves were already in the 11th century the subject of speculation and fable. There is certainly no archaeological evidence from skeletons to suggest diminutive stature. Souterrains have often been linked with the idea of living underground, but their function is now accepted as storage and their dates, where known, are pre-Pictish.

Pictish Towers

Antiquaries of the Romantic school *'found the subject-matter of their study of the past not in philosophical abstractions but in the local and particular'* (Piggott 1976,184-5), giving rise to intense interest in observable local antiquities. The popular Tours of the Scottish Highlands and Islands included ancient monuments, as did the volumes of the first *Statistical Account* compiled by local ministers in the 1790s. From at least the early 18th century into the 20th century, brochs were commonly attributed to the Picts and known as 'Pictish towers' or 'Picts' houses', though the latter term was also used to describe chambered tombs, earth-houses and indeed any underground structure. Sir Robert Sibbald wrote in 1711 of the brochs at Levenwick in Shetland as Pictish, while Cosmo Innes in 1860 wrote of *'the bell-shaped circular buildings, vulgarly called, 'Picts' Houses''*. In the 1870s, there was a notable controversy in the pages of the *Proceedings of the Society of Antiquaries of Scotland* over the question of who built the brochs, with Joseph Anderson attributing them to the Picts (as Celts) and James Fergusson to the Norsemen (1878), but supporters of the Picts won the day. Fergusson's argument rested on an extraordinary value judgement of the low level of Celtic society: the Celts, he considered, have never shown *'that steady self-reliant independence which renders the Saxon everywhere so invaluable as a colonist'* (1878, 638-9).

Although Joseph Anderson had ceased using the term 'Pictish' for brochs by the turn of the century, instead attributing them to the late Celtic period (1901,147-8), 'Pictish towers' refused to lie down; Watson's highly influential Rhind Lectures for 1916 on Scottish place-names (1926) endorsed the notion, and it survived into the 1950s in the writings of T C Lethbridge (1954,11,176). Despite the efforts of archaeologists to dispel the idea, it is still firmly rooted in popular belief. The compilers of the modern Oxford Dictionary, who define Picts as an *'ancient people of disputed origin, who formerly inhabited parts of North Britain'*, list *'Picts' houses, underground structures attributed to the Picts, found in Orkney etc'*, which displays an ignorance that cannot still be laid at the archaeologists' door as failure to communicate.

It has to be admitted that the cause of more precise terminology has been set back recently by Alfred Smyth in his book *Warlords and Holy Men* (1984,54); he argues that brochs and souterrains were Pictish because the Celtic tribes who built them were Pictish, a line of argument which is monumentally unhelpful to the archaeologist. If the term Pictish is to have any useful meaning, it must be employed not as an ethnic label but as a cultural and chronological category (Ritchie 1984,1-2). As W Douglas Simpson pointed out in his Rhind Lectures for 1941 (1943,83), *'Pict is a name without racial content'*, because Pictish blood was a mixture of the peoples who inhabited Scotland in previous generations. The real value of the classical authors' references to the Picts is to chart the political progress of the tribes of their Celtic ancestors towards the federation that became the kingdom of the Picts. If Smyth's argument was to be applied to the other end of the Pictish spectrum, one might claim that Fortrose Cathedral was built by the Picts, on the grounds that there was still Pictish blood in the population in the 13th century. As we have seen already, there was certainly an inheritance of Pictish artistic tradition at Darnaway Castle in the late 14th century, but the population had ceased to be Pictish several centuries earlier.

Perhaps it would help if we thought of Pictish as an adjective to be used in the same way as Ming of a Ming vase or Jacobean of a Jacobean tapestry. They describe a style and a period, just as Pictish symbol stone describes a particular category of stone carving. It would be a pity if historians and archaeologists could not agree on a common usage of the term, for in this period of study neither discipline can stand on its own. We all accept the round date of AD 850 as the end of the Pictish kingdom and culture; the logical beginning lies three hundred years earlier with the first historically attested king of Picts, Bridei son of Maelchon. Implicit in this definition would be the understanding that some of the artefacts and aspects of the life-style that became distinctively Pictish had been developing over previous centuries. Ian Ralston has objected very reasonably to this restricted use of the term 'Pictish' on the grounds that, in some areas such as Grampian, diagnostically Pictish houses and material culture have yet to be identified; he sees no reason why *'Pictish traits and assemblages need be distinctive archaeologically'* (1987,15). This is a valid theoretical point, but there are distinctive Pictish artefacts in Grampian, as elsewhere, in the form of symbol stones and silver chains, and there is every hope that time and funding will produce the domestic settlements to accompany Dr Ralston's own discovery of a Pictish fort at Portknockie.

Sir Walter Scott and the stature of the Picts

Sir Walter Scott visited Shetland in 1814 as the guest of a party of Commissioners for the Northern Light-House Service, and he took the opportunity to examine both the broch of Clickhimin outside Lerwick and the broch of Mousa. Scott found the situation of Clickhimin *'wild, dreary and impressive'*, and imagined that *'from the top of his tower the Pictish Monarch might look out upon a stormy sea'* (Laughlan 1982,31). On their visit to Mousa, Robert Stevenson, the famous lighthouse engineer, measured the broch and Scott recorded the details in his journal, *Northern Lights*. Scott was fascinated by the size of the galleries within the thickness of the walls of these two brochs and wrote of Mousa: *'The uppermost gallery is so narrow and low, that it was with great difficulty I crept through it'* (Laughlan 1982,47). He concluded that *'the size fully justifies the tradition prevalent here as well as in the south of Scotland, that the Picts were a diminutive race'* (Laughlan 1982,31).

The tradition that the Picts were very small was sufficiently widespread to give rise to the use of pecht, picht or pict as a *'contemptuous term for a small undersized person'* from the early 17th century onwards, and particularly in north-east Scotland into the 20th century. The *Scottish National Dictionary* records an instance in Aberdeen in 1929: *'A wee picht o' a body, he cud hae pitten her in's pooch'*. Three hundred years earlier, the Linlithgow Burgh Records for 1623 include one *'Patrik Gibbesoune, cordiner, callit the Pecht'* (*Dictionary of the Older Scottish Tongue*). It seems unlikely that such a tradition could have stemmed entirely from the *Historia Norwegiae* account mentioned already, particularly as the manuscript was discovered only in the 15th century. The idea must surely have been well entrenched in folklore from an early date. There are many stories about trolls and peerie folk in the folklore of the Northern Isles, and they were clearly thought to be small in size, dressed usually in grey, and to live inside knolls or hills (Marwick 1975,33).

The question of the racial characteristics of the Picts was taken up with relish by WC Mackenzie in a paper on 'Picts and Pets' in *The Antiquary* in 1906. Claiming that *'Antiquarian research is now conducted in a calmer and more scientific spirit'* than in the heyday of the *'Pictish controversy'*, Mackenzie argued that, as the Caledonians were *'big fair men'*, so must the Picts have been. The Scottish peasantry of his day viewed them as a small dark race, which Mackenzie explained as the result of confusion between Picts and Pets. The Pets or Peti were the dwarfish people described in the *Historia Norwegiae*, to be found in the Northern Isles and Caithness, and Mackenzie considered them to have racial affinities with the Lapps. Contemporary popular tradition held the Lapps to be notably small people.

If you ask people in Scotland today how they think of the Picts, opinion seems to be divided between red and dark hair but united on small size!

John Buchan and the Picts of Galloway

The Picts have rarely figured in novels or short stories, but they appear to considerable effect in one of John Buchan's tales of Scotland, No-Man's-Land. Buchan spent walking holidays in Galloway and must have absorbed not only the landscape and atmosphere of south-west Scotland but also local traditions about the Picts of Galloway. The hero of the story, Mr Graves, Fellow of St Chad's, Oxford, is fascinated by *'the ancient life of the North, of the Celts and the Northmen and the unknown Pictish tribes'* (Buchan 1902,4) and sets off alone to explore *'the cold brown hills'* of Galloway. He muses on the origins of the Picts, whom he finds *'a sort of blank wall to put an end to speculation'*, and remembers a student of his at St Chad's who was convinced that the Picts still lived in the Allermuir hills. After a day's fishing in the hills, the mist comes down and Mr Graves loses his way.

'Then suddenly in the hollow trough of mist before me, where things could still be half-discerned, there appeared a figure. It was little and squat and dark; naked, apparently, but so rough with hair that it wore the appearance of a skin-covered being. It crossed my line of vision, not staying for a moment, but in its face and eyes there seemed to lurk an elder world of mystery and barbarism, a troll-like life which was too horrible for words' (Buchan 1902,38).

This story was written while Buchan was at Oxford in the 1890s - his literary earnings helped to pay his way at Brasenose College - and was published in *The Watcher by the Threshold and Other Tales* in 1902 (Smith 1979,27). It was reprinted after his death in *Famous Fantastic Mysteries* in 1949, and Buchan's Pict was there illustrated by Leydenfrost as a ferocious hairy being (Smith 1979,79) (fig. 13).

The question of the Picts of Galloway is a fine red herring that originated in the 12th century and has persisted into the 20th century. It has been fully researched and discussed by John MacQueen in the course of his work on St Ninian (1990), and he has shown that the tradition arose out of a series of misunderstandings by four English writers of the 12th century, Reginald of Durham, Jocelin of Furness and Richard and John of Hexham. Richard Oram has attributed the origin of the tradition of Galloway Picts specifically to Richard of Hexham, arguing that Richard was seeking by the use of the term Picts to show his deep knowledge of the history of northern Britain (1993, 26).

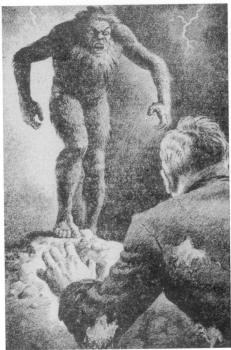

Fig. 13. John Buchan's Galloway Pict by Leydenfrost illustrating the story 'No-Man's-Land'.

Heather Ale

One of Mr Graves' discoveries about the latter-day Picts of Galloway was that they still made heather ale, *'that lost delicacy of the North'*. Heather ale and the story of how the recipe was lost were made famous by Robert Louis Stevenson's ballad, 'Heather Ale, a Galloway Legend':

'From the bonny bells of heather
They brewed a drink long-syne,
Was sweeter far than honey,
Was stronger far than wine.
They brewed it and they drank it,
And lay in a blessed swound,
For days and days together
In their dwellings underground.'

Ernest Marwick recorded that the story of heather ale was known orally in the Northern Isles until modern times, but he commented that it was difficult to decide whether any real tradition lay behind them, because they have a *'suspiciously 'bookish' quality' about them'* (1975,63). The story tells how the last of the old race to know the recipe were a father and son, who were caught by Viking invaders; the father agreed to divulge the precious secret on condition that his son was not present to hear his treachery. The Vikings promptly killed the son, whereupon the father explained that torture might have wrung the secret from his son - but he himself would never tell. In the Galloway legend, the persecutor is a Scottish king but the story is the same, and the secret dies with the *'last of the dwarfish men'*. Another version of the same legend occurs in Ireland in connection with Viking beer.

In Orkney there used to be a very common wild oat grass which was known as 'Pight aits' and which was made both into bread and into *'an excellent ale which never caused drunkenness'*. There was also an Orcadian recipe using young green heather-tops which existed at least until the late 19th century. A similar brew was noted in Islay in 1772 by Pennant (1776,262): *'Ale is frequently made in this island of the young tops of heaths, mixing two thirds of that plant with one of malt, sometimes adding hops'*. A Highland recipe was used by Bruce Williams to produce heather ale, named Leann Fraoch, commercially in 1993 in Glasgow.

Current perception of the Picts

The modern view of the Picts, as of their contemporary neighbours, is dominated by two popular images, those of heroic society and of holy men in retreat from that society. As Wendy Davies has argued

(1984), neither image is very helpful and together they obscure the bulk of the population whose major concern was neither glory on the battlefield nor sainthood but the arduous business of making a living. Artefact studies underline the similarities between the material culture of the Picts and Scots, and, while they spoke different versions of the Celtic language, there are no longer strong enough reasons to believe that the Picts had a second, non-Indo-European, language.

Archaeology over the last two decades has succeeded in identifying some of the settlements, forts and burials of the Picts, with the result that, as an early medieval people, they are losing their elusive quality. The evidence from new excavations has allowed the re-interpretation of old excavations of broch sites and the recognition of building sequences spanning the generations from the Picts back to their ancestors (Hedges 1990). With the help of aerial photography, it is only a matter of time and money before Pictish settlements are identified throughout mainland Scotland. There is, however, one aspect of Pictish culture that remains and will always remain unique - the symbol stones. The Picts were not alone among their contemporaries either in stone-carving or in using symbols, but no other people combined the two into such a rich and intricate system of communication. Our perception of the Picts should be of a people who were part of the community of early medieval Europe but whose life-style included a unique element that we shall probably never fully understand.

References

Allen, J R & Anderson, J 1903 *The early Christian monuments of Scotland*, Edinburgh (reprinted as a facsimile in two volumes by the Pinkfoot Press, Balgavies, 1993).

Anderson, A O & Anderson, M O 1961 *Adomnan's Life of Columba*, London.

Anderson, J 1881 *Scotland in early Christian times*, Edinburgh.

Anderson, J 1901 'Notice of nine brochs along the Caithness coast from Keiss to Skirza Head...', *Proc Soc Antiq Scot*, 35 (1900-01), 112-48.

Anderson, M O 1973 *Kings and kingship in early Scotland*, Edinburgh.

Anderson, M O 1987 'Picts - the name and the people', in Small (ed) 1987, 7-14.

Bede *A history of the English Church and people*, translated by L Sherley-Price, London, 1955.

Brown, J 1972 'Northumbria and the Book of Kells', Jarrow Lecture 1971, *Anglo-Saxon England*, 1 (1972), 219-46.

Buchan, John 1902 *The Watcher by the Threshold and Other Tales*, Blackwood, Edinburgh.

Camden, W 1789 *Britannia*, London.

Chadwick, N K 1958 'The name Pict', *Scottish Gaelic Studies*, 8 (1958), 146-76.

Chalmers, G 1807 *Caledonia*, vol 1, reprinted 1887, Edinburgh.

Childe, V G 1935 *The Prehistory of Scotland*, London.

Childe, V G 1931 *Skara Brae: a Pictish village in Orkney*, London.

Close-Brooks, Joanna 1975 'A Pictish pin from Golspie, Sutherland', *Proc Soc Antiq Scot*, 106 (1974-5), 208-10.

Close-Brooks, J 1984 'Pictish and other burials', in Friell & Watson (eds), 87-114.

Cowan, E J 1984 'Myth and identity in early medieval Scotland', *Scottish Historical Review*, 63 (1984), 111-35.

Dalrymple, J 1705 *Collections concerning the Scottish history ...*, Edinburgh.

Davies, Wendy 1984 'Picts, Scots and Britons', in Smith, LM (ed) *The making of Britain: the Dark Ages*, London, 63-76.

Driscoll, S T 1986 'Symbol stones and Pictish ethnography, review of *Symbol stones of Scotland*', *Scottish Archaeological Review*, 159-64.

Fergusson, J 1878 'On the Norwegian origin of Scottish brochs', *Proc Soc Antiq Scot*, 12 (1877-8), 630-69.

Friell, J G P and Watson, W G (eds) *Pictish Studies*, Brit Archaeol Rep, Brit Ser 125, Oxford.

Hedges, John W 1990 'Surveying the foundations: life after 'brochs'', in Armit, I (ed) *Beyond the brochs: changing perspectives on the Atlantic Scottish Iron Age*, Edinburgh, 17-31.

Henderson, Isabel 1982 'Pictish art and the Book of Kells', in Whitelock,D, McKitterick,R and Dumville,D (eds) *Ireland in early medieval Europe*, Cambridge, 79-105.

Innes, C 1860 *Scotland in the Middle Ages*, Edinburgh.

Innes, T 1729 *A critical essay on the ancient inhabitants of the northern parts of Britain, or Scotland*, London.

Jackson, A 1971 'Pictish social structure and symbol stones', *Scottish Studies*, 15(1971), 121-40.

Jackson, A 1984 *The symbol stones of Scotland*, Stromness.

Jackson, K H 1969 *The Gododdin: the oldest Scottish poem*, Edinburgh.

Laughlan, W F 1982 (ed) *Northern Lights*, by Sir Walter Scott, Byways, Hawick.

Lethbridge, T C 1954 *The Painted Men*, London.

Mann, L 1914 'The archaic sculpturings of Dumfries and Galloway', *Trans Dumfries & Galloway Nat Hist & Antiquarian Soc*, 3rd ser, 3 (1914-15), 121-66.

Mackenzie, W C 1906 'Picts and Pets', *The Antiquary*, 42 (1906), 172-5.

MacQueen, John 1990 *St Nynia*, Edinburgh.

Marwick, Ernest W 1975 *The Folklore of Orkney and Shetland*, London.

Maule, H 1706 *History of the Picts*, Edinburgh.

Oram, Richard D 1993 'The mythical Pict and the monastic pedant: the origins of the legend of the Galloway Picts', *Pictish Arts Society Journal*, 4 (1993), 14-27.

Piggott, S 1976 *Ruins in a landscape*, Edinburgh.

Piggott, Stuart 1989 *Ancient Britons and the Antiquarian Tradition*, London, 1989.

Radcliffe-Brown, A R 1952 *Structure and function in primitive society*, London.

Ralston, Ian 1987 'Portknockie: promontory forts and Pictish settlement in the north-east', in Small (ed) 1987, 15-26.

Ritchie, A 1983 'Birsay around AD 800', *Orkney Heritage*, 2 (1983), 46-66.

Ritchie, A 1984 'The archaeology of the Picts: some current problems', in Friell & Watson (eds) 1984, 1-6.

Ritson, J 1828 *Annals of the Caledonians, Picts and Scots ...*, Edinburgh.

Royal Commission on the Ancient and Historical Monuments of Scotland 1984 *Argyll 5, Islay, Jura, Colonsay and Oronsay*, Edinburgh.

Sibbald, Sir R 1711 *Description of the Isles of Orkney and Zetland*, Edinburgh.

Simpson, W Douglas 1943 *The province of Mar*, Aberdeen.

Small, A (ed) *The Picts: a new look at old problems*, Dundee.

Smith, J A 1873 'Notice of ... ancient Scottish silver chains', *Proc Soc Antiq Scot*, 10(1872-3), 321-47.

Smith, Janet Adam 1979 *John Buchan and his world*, Thames and Hudson, London.

Smyth, A 1984 *Warlords and holy men: Scotland AD 80-1000*, Edinburgh.

Southesk, Earl of 1893 *Origins of Pictish symbolism*, Edinburgh.

Spearman, R Michael and Higgitt, John 1993 *The Age of Migrating Ideas*, Edinburgh.

Stell, G & Baillie, M 1993 'The Great Hall and roof of Darnaway Castle, Moray', in Sellar, WDH (ed) *Moray: province and people*, Edinburgh, 162-86.

Stuart, J 1859 *Sculptured stones of Scotland*, Edinburgh.

Thomas, C 1964 'The interpretation of the Pictish symbols', *Archaeol Journal*, 120 (1964), 31-97.

Thomson, W P L 1986 'St Findan and the Pictish-Norse transition', in Berry, RJ & Firth, HN (eds) *The People of Orkney*, Kirkwall, 279-83.

Wainwright, F T 1955 *The Problem of the Picts*, Edinburgh.

Walker, J 1804 'On the antient Camelon, and the Picts', *Archaeologia*, 1 (1804), 252-9.

Watkins, T 1984 'Where were the Picts? An essay in settlement archaeology,' in Friell & Watson (eds), 63-86.

Watson, W J 1926 *Celtic Place Names of Scotland*, Edinburgh.

Wilson 1851 *The archaeology and prehistoric annals of Scotland*, Edinburgh.

Youngs, Susan (ed) 1989 *'The work of angels'*, London.